PINK FLOYD

PINK FLOYD

Edited by
MARCUS HEARN

Designed by
PERI GODBOLD

Reynolds & Hearn Ltd
London

For Doug, crazy diamond

First published in 2008 by
Reynolds & Hearn Ltd
61a Priory Road
Kew Gardens
Richmond
Surrey
TW9 3DH

Images © Rex Features 2008
Text © Marcus Hearn 2008

A CIP catalogue record for this book is available from the British Library.

ISBN 978 1 905287 82 6 Paper Back
ISBN 978 1 905287 49 9 Hard Back

Printed and bound in India by Replika Press.

INTRODUCTION

Charting the history of Pink Floyd, the world's best-loved art rock group, poses a considerable challenge for the prospective biographer; these five musicians traced a circuitous and unorthodox path from humble beginnings in 1965 to a redemptive reunion some 40 years later.

There is of course not one, but at least three Pink Floyds – the experimental psychedelia of the 1960s gave way to introspective concept albums in the 1970s and stadium pageantry in the 1980s. A remarkably consistent strain of English melancholy suffused all the different phases of the group, who for much of their existence were motivated by bass player Roger Waters' desire to extend the boundaries of popular music and live performance. As early as 1969 he declared, 'We could go on doing the same old numbers which are very popular and we would enjoy doing it, but that's not what the Pink Floyd is all about. It's about taking risks and pushing forward.'

This book is not an exhaustive chronicle of the last five decades, but a history based on highlights from the photographs archived by Rex Features. Even here, however, the task proved to be far from straightforward, due in large part to the band's reclusive nature. When Pink Floyd re-emerged in 1980 following one of their fallow periods, Roger Waters discovered that 'there was a mystique which had grown up around us. We started enjoying the mystery. It's very nice; nobody knows who we are. I can walk around backstage, and nobody recognises me. I can even walk out into the audience. It's great.'

The group were not only absent from their album sleeves for most of their career, but managed to avoid being photographed at almost any public event that wasn't a Pink Floyd concert. And even on stage they retreated behind bizarre props, dazzling lights and mesmerising film shows. Partly as a result of this, *Rex Collections: Pink Floyd* is dominated by shots of the band's constantly evolving stage shows.

The legendary Syd Barrett created the group that he christened by combining the names of Georgia blues men Pink Anderson and Floyd 'Dipper Boy' Council. His rise to prominence and tragic decline is depicted in the photographs that show his transition from fresh-faced optimism to bewildered despair.

Perhaps mindful of the music industry pressures that had contributed to their friend's demise, the remaining members of Pink Floyd gradually eschewed the trappings of pop stardom. The photographs from the late 1960s to the 1970s show Pink Floyd swapping garish satin frills for jeans, t-shirts, and the ultimate anonymity of hiding from their audience behind a huge wall. The album *The Dark Side of the Moon* and subsequent songs such as 'Have a Cigar' made it clear that they were all too wary of the consequences of playing the game.

From the *Wall* shows of 1980 and 1981 the performance photographs depict a group who seemingly only want to be perceived in terms of the theatrical distractions they offered to their audiences. One suspects that the return of posed band shots in the late 1980s had more to do with the rancorous split with Roger Waters than any desire on the part of David Gilmour, Nick Mason and Richard Wright to seek self-publicity. The shots of the three-man line up that appear towards the end of the book were possibly taken to remind the public that Pink Floyd could still progress, and indeed exist, without Waters' permission or guidance.

Perhaps the most remarkable page in the book is the one depicting the climax of Pink Floyd's reunion performance at Live 8 in July 2005. The shot of Gilmour, Waters, Mason and Wright bidding farewell to their audience (possibly for the last time) is similar to countless pictures of other groups taking their bows at the end of a concert, but the 24 years of bickering and animosity that preceded this moment lend this image a special poignancy.

Some of the leading photographers represented in this collection include Harry Goodwin, Dezo Hoffman and Marc Sharratt, whose early portraits of the group represent the very best that traditional and experimental pop photography had to offer in the 1960s. Ray Stevenson and Nik Wheeler's intimate live shots are highlights of subsequent sections, while André Csillag, Stephen Meddle and Brian Rasic step back from the spectacle to portray the band's seemingly incidental role in their own stage shows.

As ever, thanks are due to the librarians and other staff at Rex Features, and especially to New Business Manager Glen Marks. We are also grateful to Andrew Godfrey for additional scanning and diligent image restoration.

The events of 2005 proved that commentators would be unwise to assume that the final chapter in Pink Floyd's history has been written. This book offers a visual document of the story so far: a journey of remarkable musical achievements and all-too-human frailties.

Roger Keith 'Syd' Barrett was born in Cambridge on 6 January 1946. Pink Floyd's original singer, guitarist and creative leader, Barrett wrote the songs which transformed his group from a covers band to pioneers of the new 'psychedelic' sound. In the *Melody Maker* of 1 April 1967, Barrett defended the band's first single, 'Arnold Layne', a cheeky record about a Cambridge transvestite who stole underwear from washing lines. 'Arnold Layne just happens to dig dressing up in women's clothing. A lot of people do – let's face up to reality.'

Barrett seemed unconcerned that Radio London had recently banned the 'smutty' disc. 'If more people like them dislike us, more people like the underground lot are going to dig us, so we hope they'll cancel each other out.'

PHOTOGRAPHS: Harry Goodwin

George Roger Waters was born in Great Bookham, Surrey, on 6 September 1943. Roger's father was killed in action in 1944, and the family moved to Cambridge soon after.

Waters was 13 when he first heard Ray Charles singing 'Georgia On My Mind', by Hoagy Carmichael. 'I remember thinking, if I could write one song like that, it would make me happier than anything else in life.'

Waters met Barrett at a Saturday morning art class in Cambridge, but Pink Floyd would coalesce in London when Waters was studying architecture alongside Nick Mason and Rick Wright at Regent Street Polytechnic. By 1966 Waters had settled on the roles of bass player and occasional singer in the band.

'I could have been an architect,' said Waters in 1970, 'but I don't think I would have been very happy. Nearly all modern architecture is a silly game as far as I can see. I'm happier the way I am, and I can always build a house for myself one day if I want to.'

PHOTOGRAPHS: Harry Goodwin

Nicholas Berkeley Mason, the group's drummer, was born in Birmingham on 27 January 1945. Mason now admits that not every member of Pink Floyd shared Barrett's enthusiasm for the so-called Summer of Love. 'We were very much right place, right time,' said Mason in 2003. 'When everyone else was enjoying these happenings we were probably halfway back to Manchester on the M1. I think Syd was part of it but the rest of us were just college kids. We weren't working at it or deep in it.'

In the turbulent years to come, the steadfast Mason would prove to be the only member of the group to play on every Pink Floyd album.

PHOTOGRAPHS: Harry Goodwin

Richard William Wright was born in Pinner, London, on 28 July 1945. The group's keyboard player and co-singer, and the most musically accomplished member of the original line-up, Wright would help with arrangements and occasionally tune Waters' bass.

Wright was the shyest member of the group, but he nevertheless joined Barrett's defence of 'Arnold Layne' when interviewed by *Melody Maker*. 'I think the record was banned not because of the lyrics, because there's nothing there you can really object to, but because they're against us as a group and against what we stand for.'

PHOTOGRAPH: Harry Goodwin

Pink Floyd soon became the darlings of the psychedelic underground, so it was not without some controversy that they signed to EMI in February 1967. This sequence of pictures was taken on Saturday 1 April 1967, the day the group were formally unveiled to the press with an awkwardly staged mock performance, during which Barrett posed with the Danelectro guitar he had bought with his advance. Later that afternoon there were high jinks on the pavement outside EMI's office in Manchester Square, London.

In early July the band went national when they made their first appearance on the BBC television programme *Top of the Pops*, miming to their second single 'See Emily Play'. Later that month, on the TV show *Juke Box Jury*, disc jockey Pete Murray dismissed the group as 'a con'.

The first Pink Floyd album, *The Piper at the Gates of Dawn*, was released on 5 August 1967. It had taken five months to record and mix – not quite unprecedented in the era of studio experimentation pioneered by The Beatles, but nonetheless an unusually lengthy period for such a new group. One of the most influential LPs released during a crucial year for the burgeoning counter-culture, *Piper* remains highly regarded today.

PHOTOGRAPHS: Dezo Hoffman

TRI-X PAN FILM

KODAK SAF.ETY FILM ▲●

AF.ETY FILM ▲●

KODAK TRI-X

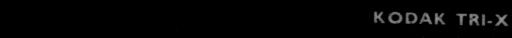

PAGES 25-29

Aware of Pink Floyd's reputation for live 'freak outs' and 'trippy' light shows, photographers experimented using filters and various distortion techniques in an effort to create a visual representation of the new psychedelic sound. Vic Singh created a striking montage of the group for *The Piper at the Gates of Dawn*, one of the few Floyd LPs to feature discernible portraits of the band-members on its front cover. Earlier in 1967 Rex photographer Marc Sharratt had adopted his own approach, as this sequence of pictures illustrates.

PHOTOGRAPHS: Marc Sharratt

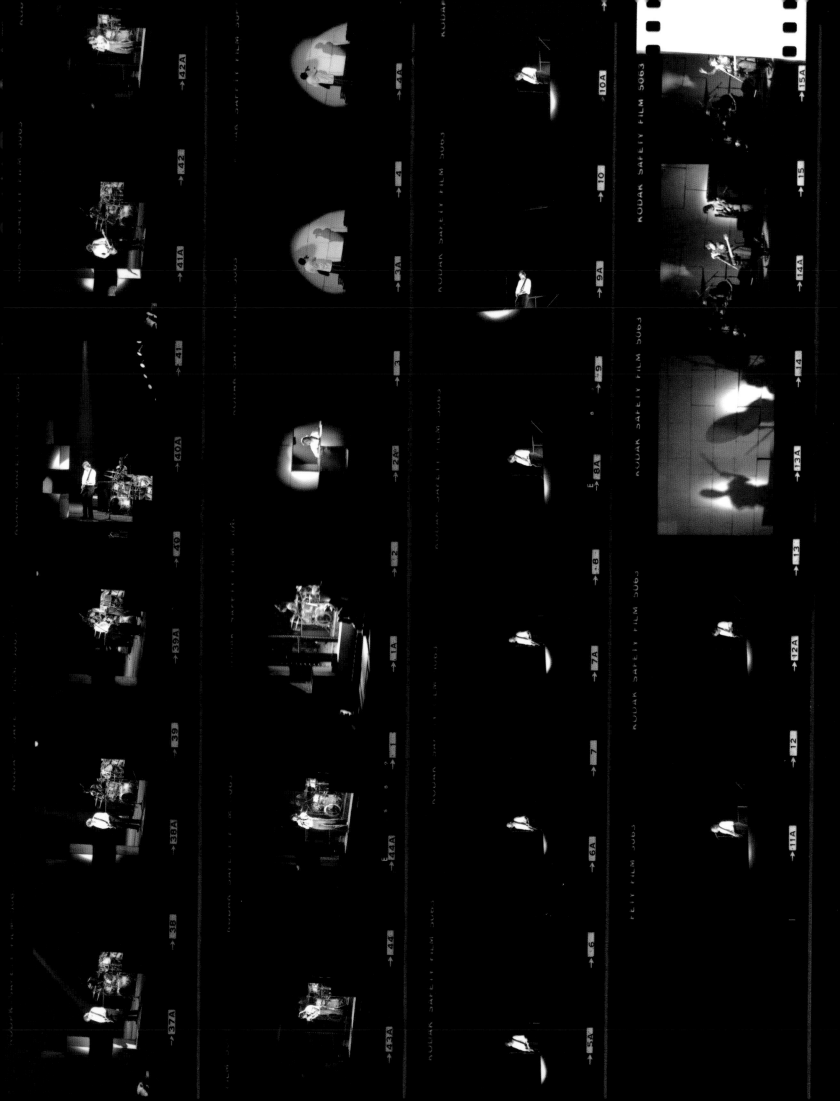

The second half of 1967 saw Pink Floyd build on the success of *The Piper at the Gates of Dawn* and some rapturously received London shows. Audiences in the provinces reacted with bemusement or hostility towards the group's extended psychedelic jams and belligerent refusal to play their singles, but a tireless touring schedule ensured that their following steadily grew.

'We write our own material and don't just record other people's numbers or copy American demo discs,' boasted Nick Mason in 1967. 'Our album shows parts of the Pink Floyd that haven't been heard yet.'

Syd Barrett claimed: 'It all comes straight out of our heads and it isn't too far out to understand. If we play well on stage I think most people understand that what we play isn't just a noise. Most audiences respond to a good set.'

By autumn 1967, the only thing that threatened Pink Floyd's trajectory was Barrett's prodigious consumption of mind-altering drugs. The chemicals that had been the catalyst for his songwriting genius were now taking him to the brink of a mental breakdown.

PHOTOGRAPHS: Dezo Hoffman

A dishevelled Syd Barrett performed his last major gig with Pink Floyd at 'Christmas on Earth Continued', an all-night extravaganza held at Olympia in London on 22 December 1967. Pink Floyd shared the bill with The Jimi Hendrix Experience, The Who, Eric Burdon & The Animals, The Move and numerous other groups. The Floyd's performance at this landmark event was filmed but the footage has never been released.

PHOTOGRAPH: Ray Stevenson

As Pink Floyd became more successful Syd Barrett became increasingly erratic and unreliable. In August 1967 a group spokesman had explained Barrett's intermittent absences from shows by saying that he was suffering from 'nervous exhaustion', but Syd's mental health problems were far more serious.

The final straw came at the end of the year when Barrett informed his band-mates that Pink Floyd should be augmented by (according to various accounts) two saxophonists, a banjo player and a female singer. The group devised an ill-fated scheme to retain Barrett in a songwriting capacity, in much the same way that the Beach Boys regarded the similarly fragile Brian Wilson, while they searched for someone to replace their former leader for live performances.

PHOTOGRAPH: Percy Hatchman

Syd Barrett's replacement in Pink Floyd was David Jon Gilmour. Born in Cambridge on 6 March 1946, guitarist and lead vocalist Gilmour had been a friend of Barrett's in Cambridge since he was 15, and had supported Pink Floyd on numerous occasions as a member of Jokers Wild. Gilmour had been invited to the recording of 'See Emily Play', and had been shocked by the way the unravelling Barrett had blanked him.

The first of these shots was taken in May 1968, but Gilmour had rehearsed with a short-lived five-man line-up of the group as early as January.

'Following someone like Syd Barrett into the band was a strange experience,' said Gilmour in 1973. 'At first I felt I had to change a lot and it was a paranoiac experience. After all, Syd was a living legend, and I had started off playing basic rock music – Beach Boys, Bo Diddley, and 'The Midnight Hour'. I wasn't in any groups worth talking about.

'It took me a long time to feel part of the band after Syd left. It was such a strange band, and very difficult for me to know what we were doing. People were very down on us after Syd left. Everyone thought Syd was all the group had, and dismissed us.'

PHOTOGRAPHS: Ray Stevenson

pages 40-45

The second Pink Floyd album, *A Saucerful of Secrets*, was released on 29 June 1968. On the same day the group topped the bill at 'Midsummer High', a free concert at the Cockpit in London's Hyde Park. The band was supported by Tyrannosaurus Rex and Jethro Tull, and at one point were joined by their friend and later collaborator Roy Harper, who is captured in Ray Stevenson's dynamic photographs. These shots also illustrate the cramped conditions on the stage, which was just six inches off the ground.

Radio 1 disc jockey John Peel subsequently described the event as 'the nicest concert I've ever been to. I hired a boat and rowed out, and I lay on the bottom of the boat, in the middle of the Serpentine, and just listened to the band play and their music then, I think, suited the open air perfectly… They just seemed to fill the whole sky.'

Midsummer High marked a turning point for Pink Floyd – the event was a public declaration of intent for the group's new line-up, and would prove to be the first of several legendary free concerts in Hyde Park.

PHOTOGRAPHS: Ray Stevenson

The double LP *Ummagumma* was released in October 1969 and reflected Pink Floyd's rather directionless state. Sides one and two featured live performances from the previous June, while sides three and four offered largely impenetrable solo compositions from each band-member. Rick Wright's 'Sysyphus' opened the group's show at the Royal Albert Hall on 7 February 1970, and was singled out for criticism by the *Melody Maker*'s Richard Williams, who complained that the song's opening and closing theme arrangements were 'almost ruined by David Gilmour's slipshod pitching, and an apparently unconscious disagreement over time between Roger Waters, Nick Mason and Wright, all of whose downbeats arrived separately like raindrops in a barrel.'

There was better to come later in the evening, with more compelling renditions of 'Set the Controls for the Heart of the Sun' and 'A Saucerful of Secrets'.

PHOTOGRAPH: Ray Stevenson

On 28 June 1970 the group appeared at the Holland Pop Festival 70 at Krallingse Bod, Rotterdam. By this stage in the development of the live show only 'Astronomy Domine' and 'Interstellar Overdrive' survived from *The Piper at the Gates of Dawn*, although the band had yet to escape the influence of Barrett by defining a popular new style.

The show also included a rendition of 'Atom Heart Mother', the lengthy and dramatic title track from the band's forthcoming album. On this occasion, however, the song was performed without the orchestral and choral backing integral to the studio recording.

'I'm bored with most of the stuff we play,' said Roger Waters later in the year. 'I'm not bored with 'Atom Heart Mother' when we get the brass and choir together, because it's so weird doing it… I'm beginning to come to a position now where I don't think we ought to play any more on a kind of Heath Robinson level – go and do it, play the numbers, do the stuff, get the money and go home… It's a job, a fucking well paid job, with all the ego boosting stuff and everything, but I think it becomes very mechanical.'

PHOTOGRAPH: Constantin

Pink Floyd performed another no frills version of 'Atom Heart Mother' when they played the 'Garden Party' at the Crystal Palace Bowl on 15 May 1971. Reviewers were critical of the band's rendition of 'Atom Heart Mother', drawing unfavourable comparisons with the version that had appeared on the eponymous album the previous October. The audience, which included photographer Dezo Hoffman, also had to contend with a prolonged downpour soon after the song began. Those unhappy with the weather found consolation in the fireworks, coloured smoke and the 60-foot inflatable octopus which rose out of the lake in front of the stage.

Musical highlights included a performance of the rarity 'Embryo' and an early airing of 'The Return of the Son of Nothing'. A week before the Crystal Palace gig Rick Wright told *Melody Maker*: 'We went into the studio in January to put down a lot of ideas and called them all bits of nothing, which is where the title came from. It's 22 minutes long, and it's a piece which we can do live without any of the problems of 'Atom Heart Mother'.' The track would appear on the forthcoming album *Meddle* under the new title 'Echoes', and would point to a fruitful new direction for a more cohesive Pink Floyd.

PHOTOGRAPHS: Dezo Hoffman

PAGES 50-53

The following month the band commenced a European tour which included dates in France. The first three pictures in this set were taken in the grounds of the ruined Royaumont Abbey near Asnieres-sur-Oise, where the group posed with French film star Jeanne Moreau. The latter performance shots were taken at the concert inside the abbey on 15 June. The show, which was filmed by French broadcaster ORTF, included 'Cymbaline' (from the band's soundtrack to the film *More*), 'Set the Controls for the Heart of the Sun' and 'Atom Heart Mother'.

PHOTOGRAPHS: Goksin Sipahioglu

PAGES 54-55

This performance shot from 1971 illustrates how Roger Waters was becoming a dominant force within the band, both off-stage and on. 'I have great faith in giving the audiences more than music,' he said in 1970. 'There is just so much more you can do to make it a complete experience than watching four long-haired youths leaping up and down beating their banjos. Not that I'm saying that's wrong, but why not try and push yourself a bit further, why just go on doing the same thing night after night?'

PHOTOGRAPH: Ilpo Musto

PAGES 57-63

Director Adrian Maben first proposed 'a marriage between art and Pink Floyd' in 1971. Wanting to create something different from a traditional concert movie he suggested filming the group in the ancient surroundings of Pompeii, where 'the music and the silence and the empty amphitheatre would mean as much, if not more, than a million [strong] crowd.'

In October 1971 Maben and his crew spent three days filming the group in and around Pompeii. The shoot included outstanding performances of 'Echoes', 'A Saucerful of Secrets', 'One Of These Days' and 'Set the Controls for the Heart of the Sun' filmed in the virtually empty amphitheatre. Technical problems had halved Maben's shooting schedule, however, so from 13 to 21 December he filmed close ups, pick ups and various front projection shots at a television studio in Paris.

The following pictures were taken during the filming in Paris, which included complete renditions of 'Careful With That Axe Eugene' and 'Mademoiselle Nobs', a blues number performed with the help of a wailing Afghan hound called Nobs. Maben is pictured with the canine co-star in the final image.

Pink Floyd Live at Pompeii was premiered in November 1972, and is valuable record of a group at the peak of their performance powers.

PHOTOGRAPHS: Crollalanza

Pink Floyd premiered their latest work, *The Dark Side of the Moon*, in live shows performed in February 1972. A logical development of 'Echoes', the new piece would be an entire album of interlinking songs with lyrics by Roger Waters. The loose theme, or 'concept', would be the causes and consequences of madness. The spectre of the mentally ill Barrett clearly haunted the band, but the reclusive singer had helped to inspire what would become Pink Floyd's greatest critical and commercial success.

The Dark Side of the Moon was released on 24 March 1973, soon becoming one of the biggest-selling albums of all time and heralding the second major phase in the band's career. 'I think every album was a step towards *The Dark Side of the Moon*, in a sense,' claims Wright. 'We were learning all the time, the techniques of the recording, and our writing was getting better.'

Interviewed in 1973, when this picture was taken, David Gilmour described the dynamic within a band on the cusp of huge international success. 'For Roger it is more important to do things that say something. Rick is more into putting out good music and I'm in the middle with Nick. I want to do it all, but sometimes I think Roger can feel the musical content is less important and can slide around it... We're bound to argue because we are all very different. I'm sure our public image is of 100 per cent spaced out drug addicts, out of our minds on acid. People do get strange ideas about us.'

The pictures on the next six pages were taken during the band's French tour of June 1974, in which they played *The Dark Side of the Moon* in its entirety.

PHOTOGRAPHS: Omnia

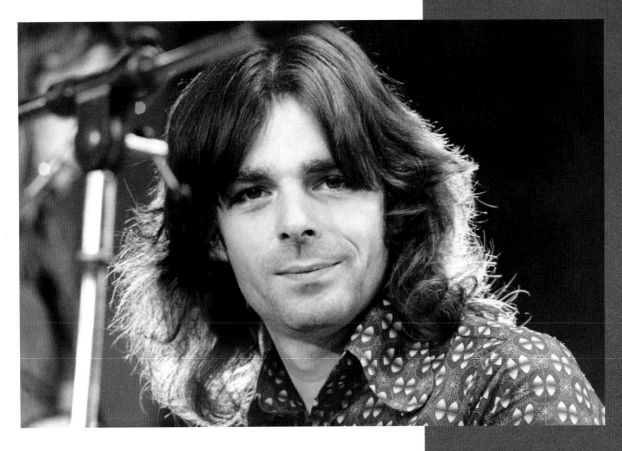

PAGES 72-90

By 1975 Pink Floyd had become a touring juggernaut accompanied by over 11 tons of equipment. That year the band played only one date in Britain, at Knebworth Park on 5 July, and used the occasion to preview tracks from their forthcoming album *Wish You Were Here*. Roger Waters introduced the epic 'Shine On You Crazy Diamond' as being 'in part about Syd Barrett, in part about rock and roll in general.'

The spectacular concert closed with what would prove to be the band's final performances of *The Dark Side of the Moon* and 'Echoes' for many years.

'We had an awful lot of problems at Knebworth,' says David Gilmour. 'Very specific problems with generator failure, and all the keyboards going out of tune. Also, we had a week to get all the equipment back from America, repaired, out to Knebworth and together for a gig which involved all our guys working day and night for three days without any sleep, and also then having to do the sound for all the other people on the gig. It was so unfortunate – we were very in practice and were playing very, very well at the time and we just got thrown.'

Despite this, the audience and critics were overwhelmed. Writing in *Sounds*, a breathless Mick Brown could barely contain his enthusiasm. 'Floyd have long since transcended the boundaries of musical definition, and their performance has been refined to the point where it is a spectacle which bombards all the senses, leaving one gasping for both air and the suitable adjectives to describe it all.'

PHOTOGRAPHS: Nik Wheeler

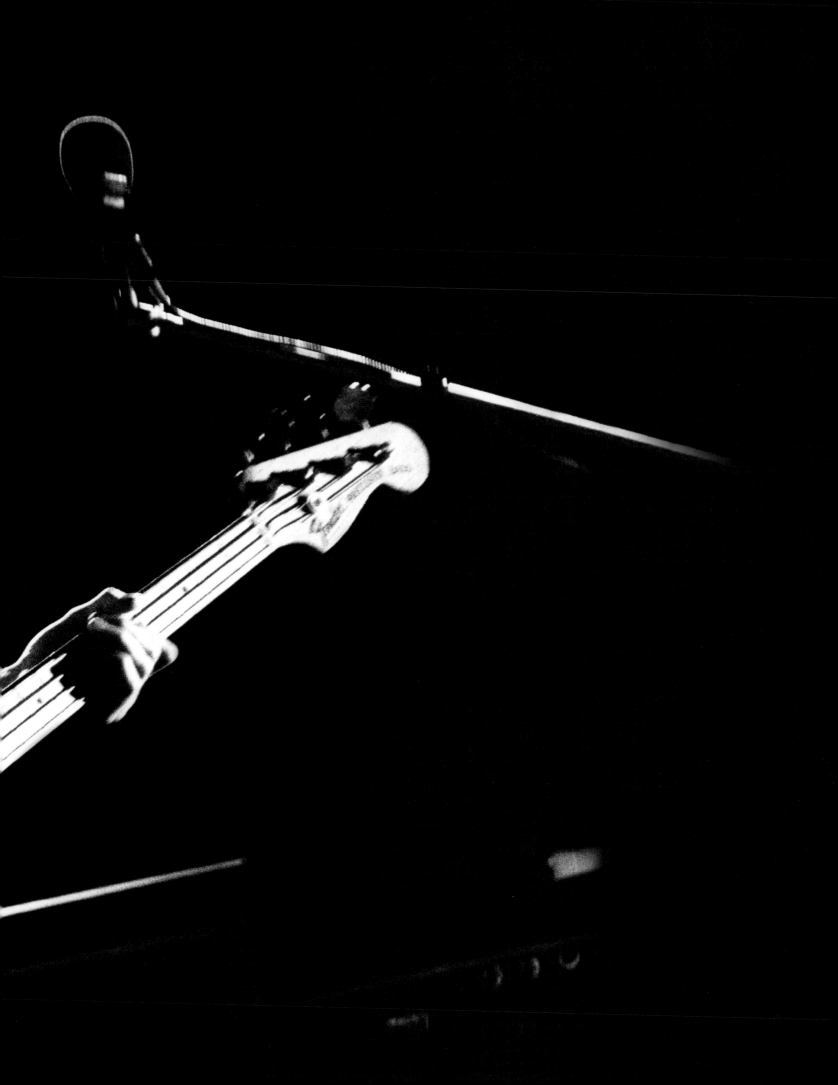

PAGES 91–105

Pink Floyd spent much of 1976 recording their latest work, a Waters-dominated concept album called *Animals*. Waters also suggested the record's striking cover, which depicted a pig flying between the towers of Battersea Power Station.

The Floyd's most aggressive-sounding record to date, *Animals* was released on 23 January 1977. On the same day the group embarked on a European tour which was rapidly followed by two gruelling tours of North America. The pictures on the following pages were taken during the band's residency at the Empire Pool, Wembley, from 15 to 19 March.

The most elaborate stage-show to date now included additional guitarist Terence 'Snowy' White (who can be seen in some of the pictures in this section) and a giant inflatable pig that was floated over the heads of the audience during performances of the *Animals* song 'Pigs'. *Melody Maker* were unimpressed by this, and the now traditional films projected on a circular screen behind the band. 'The time has come for the Pink Floyd to completely rethink their stage act. They play in vast, windy auditoria and do nothing to turn their concerts into human events: the ambience they encourage is that of a few thousand robots responding to a computer.'

Waters was similarly frustrated by the breakdown in communication between the band and its audience. His patience finally snapped during the last date of the tour, at an 80,000 capacity stadium in Montreal on 6 July. 'Halfway through I found myself spitting on one particular guy who wouldn't stop yelling. He wasn't interested in the show. None of the audience was really responding in any genuine way to what was going on onstage; they were all interested in their own performances. There was a real war going on between the musicians onstage and the audience.'

PHOTOGRAPHS: Globe, Sipa, Rex

Roger Waters' response to the spitting incident in Montreal was to explore his relationship with his audience in a new concept album called *The Wall*. The live performances of Pink Floyd's ambitious double LP would be the ultimate expression of ambitions Waters had harboured for the past decade. Rock music and theatre would dovetail in a show that saw Pink Floyd perform within, on top of and even behind a giant wall that separated them from their audience. The wall itself comprised 340 cardboard bricks which, slotted together, stretched 160 feet long and 35 feet high.

The Wall was released on 30 November 1979, and revealed that Waters was by now not only writing all the lyrics but most of Pink Floyd's music as well. 'We pretended it was a democracy for a long time,' he said in 1980, 'but this album was the era of the big own-up. It was a mildly painful experience for some of us because we have been pretending we are all jolly good chaps together. It's a load of rubbish. Ten years ago it was true, but not for the last six or seven years.'

The complexities and cost of staging *The Wall* meant that the piece was performed just 29 times. These pictures were taken from the group's shows at London's Earls Court between 4 and 9 August 1980 and 13 and 17 June 1981. For these dates the group was joined by a 'surrogate band' that included Andy Bown on bass, Snowy White on guitar, Willie Wilson on drums and Peter Wood on keyboards.

Tension during the recording of the album led to Waters dismissing Rick Wright from Pink Floyd in 1981. Wright insisted on completing the live dates, fulfilling his obligations as a session player. His departure was initially kept secret from the press, and Waters publicly insisted 'We're too lazy to split up.'

PHOTOGRAPHS: André Csillag and Brian Rasic

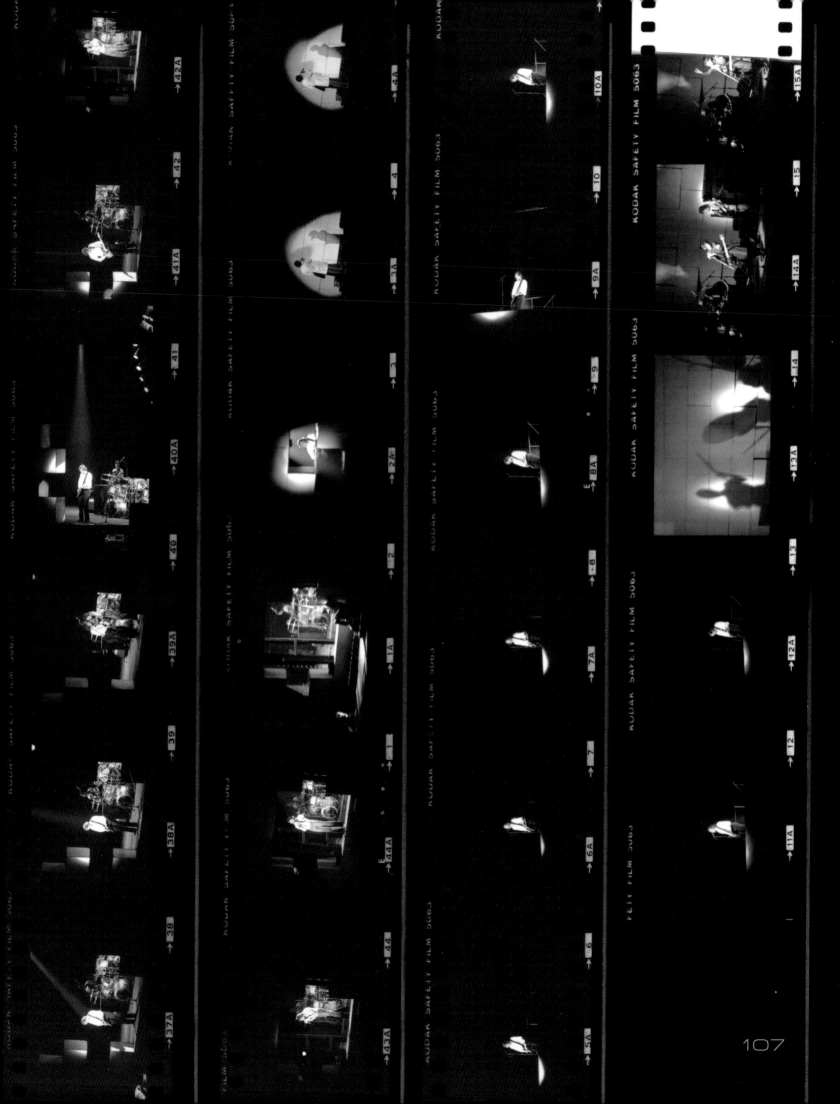

107

Pink Floyd's 1983 album *The Final Cut* was effectively a solo record from Roger Waters, who left the band two years later. Waters turned his back on the name Pink Floyd, confident that remaining members David Gilmour and Nick Mason would never use it again. 'He believed very strongly that we wouldn't do it,' said Mason in 1987. David Gilmour was rather more forthcoming about his confrontations with Waters. 'I remember meetings in which he said, "You'll never fucking do it." That's precisely what was said. Exactly that term. Except slightly harder.'

But Gilmour and Mason had other ideas. In 1986 they convened to record a new Pink Floyd album, and when Rick Wright heard about their plans he joined them.

A furious Waters, whose *Radio KAOS* album and tour would go head to head with the new Pink Floyd project, threatened numerous legal obstructions. His efforts only served to strengthen Gilmour's resolve.

PHOTOGRAPHS: Richard Young

The third phase in Pink Floyd's dramatic saga began on 8 September 1987 with the release of the new album *A Momentary Lapse of Reason*. The typically enigmatic cover featured a river of empty beds snaking into the horizon. The London press launch for the album recalled the front cover of *Animals* by floating an inflatable bed over the Thames.

PHOTOGRAPHS: Nils Jorgensen

The *Momentary Lapse of Reason* world tour began in Ontario in September 1987 and wound up in New York the following August. In 1989 the group began a European tour, dubbed 'Another Lapse', which included their first dates in the Soviet Union. At a Moscow press conference held in June (see opposite page) David Gilmour was asked about the group's acrimonious relationship with its former leader, Roger Waters. 'I don't want to talk about him,' said Gilmour. 'He is free and can do anything he wants.'

The pictures on the following pages were taken at the group's spectacular concerts at the London Arena in July. Gilmour, Mason and Wright were augmented by numerous extra musicians, including bass player Guy Pratt, keyboardist Jon Carin and guitarist Tim Renwick, an old friend of the group from Cambridge days. The set list reflected Gilmour's new dominance of the band by resurrecting tracks from *Meddle*, *The Dark Side of the Moon* and *Wish You Were Here* at the expense of anything from *Animals* and *The Final Cut*.

PHOTOGRAPHS: Steve Lewis (page 127), Fotex (page 128), Eddie Boldizsar (page 129), Brian Rasic (page 130)

Gilmour, Mason and Wright began developing ideas for the next Pink Floyd album in January 1993. Writing and recording on Gilmour's houseboat studio, *Astoria*, the trio initially worked without additional input from any other musicians. The result was arguably a more legitimate Pink Floyd album than *A Momentary Lapse*, and the group's most collaborative effort since *Wish You Were Here*.

The new album was titled *The Division Bell* (following a suggestion by author Douglas Adams), and released on 30 March 1994. The record was promoted across America by a Pink Floyd airship, at one point with Nick Mason at the controls.

In tracks such as 'Keep Talking' and the reflective 'High Hopes' *The Division Bell* conjured much of the old magic from the band's 1970s heyday. It would prove a fitting epitaph to their recording career.

PHOTOGRAPHS: Richard Young (pages 132-135), Denis Cameron (page 136)

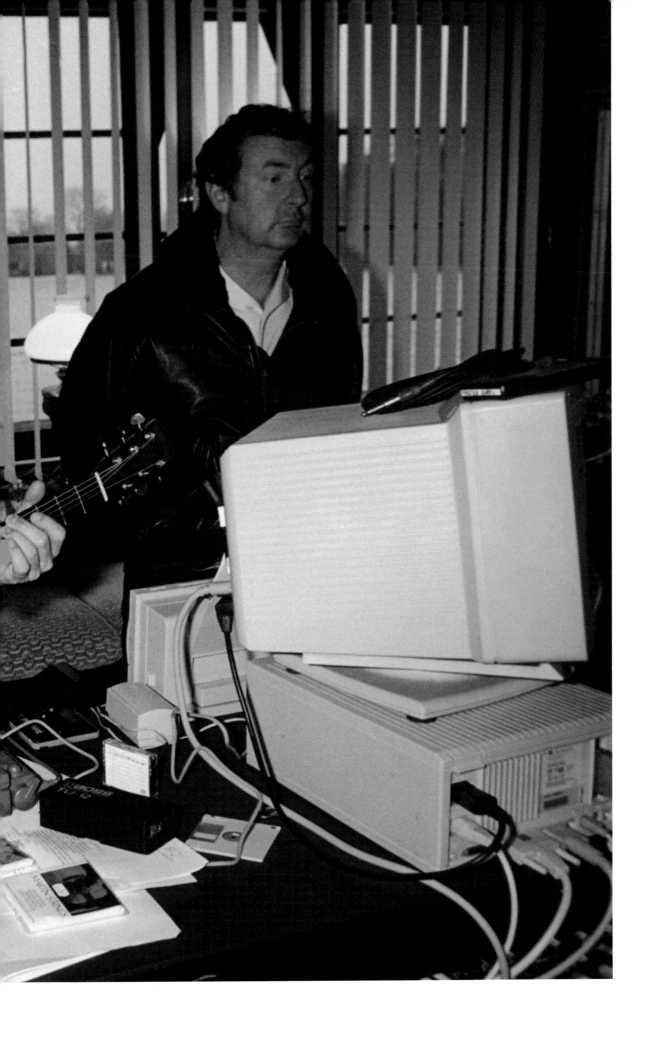

The *Division Bell* world tour spanned 17 countries and eight months, culminating in a record-breaking residency at London's Earls Court in October 1994. The pictures on these pages show the group on the steps of the venue, and performing what would prove to be their final live concerts for over a decade.

PHOTOGRAPHS: Brian Rasic (page 138), Stephen Meddle (pages 140-143)

The legal dispute between Roger Waters and Pink Floyd was settled without the ignominy of court appearances, but tit-for-tat magazine interviews prolonged the ill-feeling long after the group entered a seemingly indefinite hiatus in the mid 1990s.

On 2 July 2005 the unthinkable occurred when Bob Geldof persuaded Gilmour, Mason and Wright to join Waters for a brief set at the climax of Live 8 in Hyde Park.

Geldof regards the Pink Floyd reunion – the first time the four musicians had played together for 24 years – as an appropriate final farewell. 'A vast numberless constituency gathered about because these four men said "Enough is enough, this single thing is important enough to put behind the pathetic misgivings of the past,"' he says. 'There was nothing more potent or symbolic on that night than these four old geezers playing so beautifully, laying their own ghosts to rest.'

PHOTOGRAPHS: Richard Young (pages 144-153), Brian Rasic (pages 154-155)

Since Pink Floyd's triumphant performance at Live 8 an uneasy truce has existed between Gilmour and Waters. Events conspired against another reunion at the band's induction to the UK Music Hall of Fame on 16 November 2005. Mason and Gilmour collected the group's award at London's Alexandra Palace, but Waters' commitments to his new opera *Ça Ira* meant he appeared via a video link from Rome. Rick Wright's absence was due to illness.

PHOTOGRAPHS: David Fisher

In the wake of Live 8, and with the group remaining dormant, exactly what constituted the current line up of Pink Floyd remained unclear. On 3 July 2006 Gilmour, Mason and Wright visited London's Leicester Square for the press launch of the DVD *Pulse*, a concert film of one of the group's Earls Court performances from October 1994. In the Q&A after the brief screening, inquisitive journalists asked about the possibility of future Pink Floyd shows. While Mason and Wright expressed enthusiasm for the idea, Gilmour stated that his priority was to tour his recent solo album, *On An Island*. 'My plan is to just meander on in my own particular way for the time being.'

PHOTOGRAPH: Brian Rasic

Gilmour, Mason and Wright visited EMI's Abbey Road Studios on 4 May 2007 for a party to launch a book by Storm Thorgerson, Pink Floyd's long-standing graphic designer. Speculation about the future of the group, and possible collaborations with Roger Waters, refused to go away. In September Gilmour admitted that Live 8 'had a sense of closure… it was great to feel how that felt on that occasion with Roger there.' Since then, however, he has conceded that 'anything can happen'…

PHOTOGRAPH: Richard Young

Roger Keith Barrett passed away at his home in Cambridge on 7 July 2006. Roger's alter ego, Syd, had of course died many years before. Graffiti paying tribute to Pink Floyd's legendary lost leader appeared around the town, and flowers were left outside his gate. The card attached to the front read 'Shine on you crazy diamond. RIP Syd.'

PHOTOGRAPH: Geoff Robinson

REFERENCES

ARTICLES

Blake, Mark. 'Keep Talking'. *Q Pink Floyd Special Edition*, 2003
Boucher, Caroline. 'Waters in the Pink...' *Disc and Music Echo*, 8 August 1970
Brown, Mick. 'Floyd Fly High With Support'. *Sounds*, 12 July 1975
Fricke, David. 'Pink Floyd – The Inside Story'. *Rolling Stone*, 19 November 1987
Grausdark, Barbara, with Janet Huck. 'Up Against The Wall'. *Newsweek*, 10 March 1980
Irvin, Jim. 'A Charmed Life'. *The Word*, October 2007
Jones, Nick. 'Freaking Out With Pink Floyd'. *Melody Maker*, 1 April 1967
Mukhin, Oleg. 'The Post War Dream'. *The Amazing Pudding* Issue 54, April 1992
Walker, Dave. 'Spitfires Ahoy!'. *The Amazing Pudding* Issue 45, October 1990
Watts, Michael. 'Troubled Waters...' *Melody Maker*, 5 December 1970
Welch, Chris. 'Chris Welch Finds Out What Britain's Top "Overground" Group Are Planning'.
  Melody Maker, 3 May 1969
Welch, Chris. 'Floyd Joy'. *Melody Maker*, 19 May 1973

BOOKS

Bench, Jeff and Daniel O'Brien. *Pink Floyd's The Wall*. London: Reynolds & Hearn, 2004
Hodges, Nick and Ian Priston. *Embryo: A Pink Floyd Chronology*. London: Cherry Red Books, 1998
MacDonald, Bruno (ed). *Pink Floyd Through the Eyes of...* London: Sidgwick & Jackson, 1996
Mason, Nick. *Inside Out: A Personal History of Pink Floyd*. London: Weidenfeld & Nicolson, 2004
Miles, Barry. *Pink Floyd: A Visual Documentary*. London: Omnibus, 1988
Palacios, Julian. *Lost in the Woods: Syd Barrett and The Pink Floyd*. London: Boxtree, 1998
Povey, Glenn and Ian Russell. *Pink Floyd: In the Flesh*. London: Bloomsbury, 1997
Schaffner, Nicholas. *Saucerful of Secrets: The Pink Floyd Odyssey*. London: Sidgwick & Jackson, 1991
Watkinson, Mike and Pete Anderson. *Crazy Diamond*. London: Omnibus, 1991